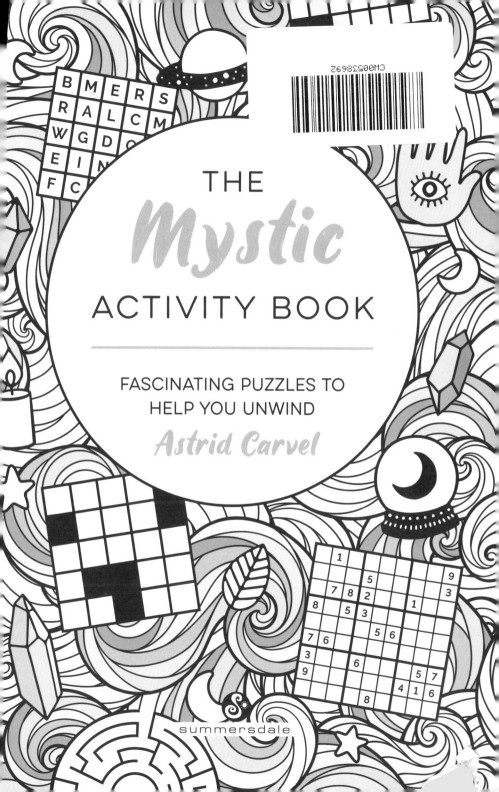

THE
Mystic
ACTIVITY BOOK

FASCINATING PUZZLES TO HELP YOU UNWIND

Astrid Carvel

summersdale

THE MYSTIC ACTIVITY BOOK

Text by Sophie Johnson

An Hachette UK Company
www.hachette.co.uk

Summersdale Publishers Ltd
Part of Octopus Publishing Group Limited
Carmelite House
50 Victoria Embankment
LONDON
EC4Y 0DZ
UK

www.summersdale.com

Printed and bound in China

ISBN: 978-1-80007-685-3

Substantial discounts on bulk quantities of Summersdale books are available to corporations, professional associations and other organizations. For details contact general enquiries: telephone: +44 (0) 1243 771107 or email: enquiries@summersdale.com.

Introduction

There's the everyday world... and then there's the otherness. This book invites you to delve into the mystical world of magick and folklore through a collection of puzzles and activities which will keep your mind as active as it is open.

Journey through crosswords, anagrams and word searches, and discover acrostics, spot the difference puzzles, word wheels and more. There are mazes to unravel, riddles to solve and beautiful mystic colouring pages to enjoy along the way. With astrology, tarot, crystals and fantastical creatures manifesting among the pages, this is no ordinary puzzle book.

So awaken your psychic senses and unleash your inner power as you explore the mystery, magnetism and magnificence of the magickal world.

Crossword

SIGNS OF THE ZODIAC

Across

2. This water sign is represented by two fish and is the final sign in the zodiac (6)

5. Represented by twins, this air sign is the third zodiacal constellation (6)

6. This water sign is represented by a sideways walker with ten legs (6)

Down

1. Characterized by a bull, this earth sign is a prominent constellation in the northern hemisphere (6)

3. This fire sign is half horse, half human and is known for its passion (11)

4. Stemming from the Latin for lion, this fire sign is known for its bravery (3)

02

Riddle

Can you solve this riddle?

We have 12 faces and 42 eyes.
We bring fortune to some
and take it from others.
Separate us, and we expire.

Word search

TAROT READING

```
H  J  E  C  I  T  S  U  J  K  A  L  K
B  I  T  R  E  S  A  Z  S  V  G  T  F
M  B  E  Y  U  J  K  L  Q  D  O  E  V
A  F  C  R  R  D  S  Z  C  I  H  M  N
G  K  I  O  O  H  G  C  R  A  D  P  P
I  K  J  R  Y  P  V  A  N  R  F  E  Z
C  U  K  E  F  A  H  L  M  E  G  R  L
I  I  K  P  T  C  S  A  C  W  V  A  O
A  C  D  M  I  J  N  H  N  O  L  N  V
N  T  D  E  X  C  F  H  I  T  L  C  E
G  R  W  S  N  G  P  B  G  D  T  E  R
H  I  G  H  P  R  I  E  S  T  E  S  S
A  G  T  G  V  C  X  S  A  U  H  J  L
```

CHARIOT	LOVERS
EMPEROR	MAGICIAN
HIEROPHANT	TEMPERANCE
HIGH PRIESTESS	TOWER
JUSTICE	

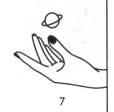

Spot the difference

04

Can you spot five differences between the two pictures?

Acrostics

Solve the clues correctly, and the shaded squares will remind you that you reap what you sow.

1. Short Japanese poem

2. A practice of focussing the mind

3. Good chance that can be foretold

4. Purple quartz crystal

5. The scales sign of the zodiac

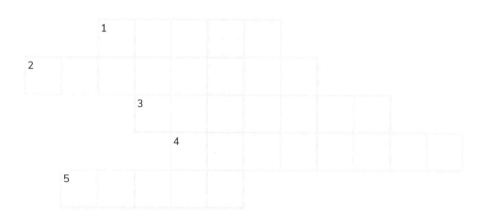

Word ladder

Change one letter at a time to turn the word **STAR** into **DUST**.

STAR

DUST

Anagrams

Rearrange these letters to reveal five crystals.

MYTH EAST

TANGER

EEL INSET

RICE TIN

OUTLIER MAN

Pairs

Match up the celestial symbols. The first pair has been done for you.

Maze

Find the right path to locate the candle at the centre of the maze.

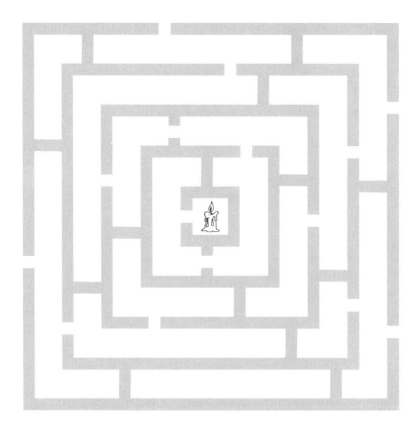

+ 水 + ॐ = 30

 + 水 - ॐ = 20

 - 水 = 5

 - ॐ + 水 = _____

Complete the following grid by filling in the empty boxes with the missing numbers. Each number can only appear once in a row, column or box.

		1			2	5	8	
			1	4	8		7	
3	8		6	9	5		1	
	9				7	3	6	2
	3	6	8		4	9	5	7
		2	9		6	1	4	
				8	9		2	
2		8	7			4	9	5
7	4	9		5	1	8	3	

Missing link

Fill in the blank spaces to make two compound words or phrases.

DEATH		BONE
LUCID		CATCHER
RED		EARTH

Hidden word

Can you find the nine-letter word hidden in the grid?

P	R	H
S	O	C
O	E	O

Let your inner light shine

Word wheel

See how many words of four or more letters you can make, using each letter only once. Each word must use the central letter. Can you find a word that uses all of the letters?

Word ladder

FULL

MOON

Change one letter at a time to turn the word **FULL** into **MOON**.

Word search

DREAM INTERPRETATION

```
A G C V F R D G J N D A S
I X F N U H E R U L I A F
N E F G O J U K L M N B V
F D E F A L L I N G K M C
I F C X S E W A S D F C H
D B E I N G C H A S E D I
E G X C D S W G K J H B L
L T A C F D N S C L M N D
I G M C D I W H J P L K H
T V S T Y D A S F O H J O
Y G F L X N J U I Y T E O
O F F P G N M H K A L J D
H T E E T G N I S O L I K
```

CHILDHOOD

FLYING

BEING CHASED

INFIDELITY

CHANGE

LOSING TEETH

EXAMS

FALLING

FAILURE

Acrostics

Solve the clues correctly, and the shaded squares will reveal a little magic.

1. Witches and fishermen both do it

2. Arachnid that extrudes silk

3. Cars that run without petrol or diesel

4. Mary Poppins' favourite mode of transport

5. A nice cackle

Hidden word

Can you find the nine-letter word hidden in the grid?

B	L	A
R	E	T
I	H	S

Sudoku

Complete the following grid by filling in the empty boxes with the missing numbers. Each number can only appear once in a row, column or box.

6				2			9	3
		5		1			2	4
4	2	8	3	5	9	1	7	6
	5	6				9	3	7
9	7	4		3				8
	3	1	9	7				
	8	3	2					1
1		2	5	4	3	7		
7					1	3		

Crossword

CRYSTALS

Across

2. A green crystal that brings good luck to those who wear it (4)

4. Popular purple crystal that eases anxiety and helps you sleep (8)

5. A dark, absorbent crystal said to soak up negative energy (5, 10)

6. A bright yellow quartz variety said to help with confidence (7)

Down

1. A pearly white, aura-cleansing crystal that dissolves in water (8)

3. This pink crystal is used for manifesting love and new relationships (4, 6)

Maze

Can you help the spider
get to the web?

A

B

C

Word ladder

WILD

CARD

Change one letter at a
time to turn the word
WILD into **CARD**.

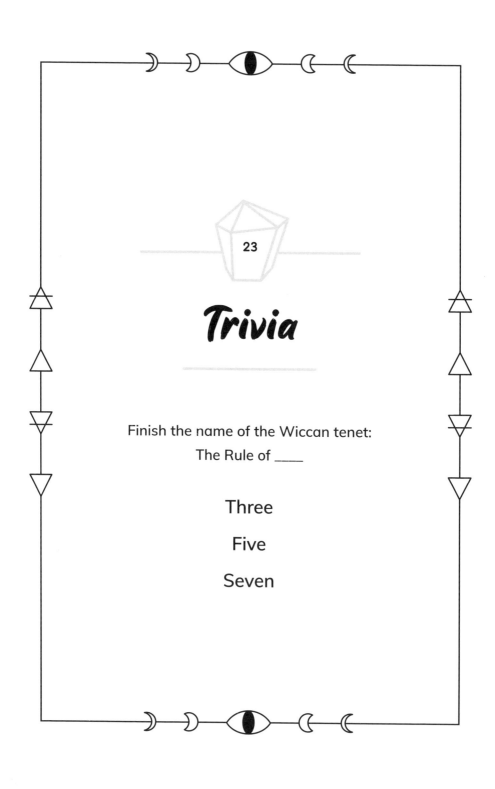

Trivia

Finish the name of the Wiccan tenet:
The Rule of ____

Three

Five

Seven

Spot the difference

Can you spot five differences between the two pictures?

Counting conundrum

♏ × ♋ = 72

♋ × ♎ = 36

♏ × ♎ = 32

♏ = ___   ♋ = ___   ♎ = ___

Anagrams

Rearrange these letters to reveal five things to do with spellcasting.

DUAL CORN _____

SHREB _____

LATAR _____

MAG PARENT _____

NIP TOO _____

Pairs

Match up these pairs of owls. The first one has been done for you.

Word ladder

Change one letter at a time to turn the word **TAROT** into **CARDS**.

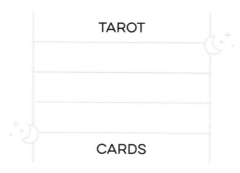

TAROT

CARDS

Anagrams

Rearrange these letters to reveal the five Wiccan elements.

RIA

PI STIR

WE RAT

HEART

RIFE

Word wheel

See how many words of four or more letters you can make, using each letter only once. Each word must use the central letter. Can you find a word that uses all of the letters?

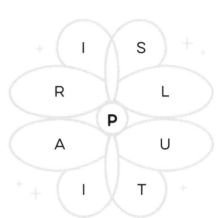

Word ladder

SLEEP

DREAM

Change one letter at a time to turn the word **SLEEP** into **DREAM**.

Counting conundrum

$$\text{scroll} + \text{scroll} + \text{scroll} = 30$$

$$\text{scroll} + \text{candle} + \text{candle} = 20$$

$$\text{candle} + \text{leaf} + \text{leaf} = 13$$

$$\text{scroll} + (\text{candle} \times \text{leaf}) = \underline{\hspace{3cm}}$$

Sudoku

Complete the following grid by filling in the empty boxes with the missing numbers. Each number can only appear once in a row, column or box.

	7	3		9			8	
	8				7			9
	5		6				2	3
				1	5	3		
3	6	1			9		5	2
7		5	3	2			9	8
	1	7	9				3	
6		8		4	2	9		5
5		2	1	6				

Crossword

BIRTH CHARTS

Across

3. Each chart is divided into twelve _____ (6)

4. Which satellite of Earth features in a birth chart? (4)

6. Your birth chart shows which sign of the _____ you are (6)

Down

1. The position of this planet indicates how you give and fall in love (5)

2. The word for the study of celestial bodies that inform our lives (9)

5. This planet's position hints at your sex drive, energy and passion (4)

Spot the difference

Can you spot five differences between the two pictures?

Maze

Find the right path to locate the feather at the centre of the maze.

Word search

DARK ARTS

```
M H B F O R B I D D E N M
A Y L J D V C F R E O D J
L Z Y H G E F R D S A Z C
E H Y J A K M L I J N B V
F Y G V C C K O H B V C S
I X S G H Y P D N J A X A
C Z M N B H Y G D I G Y C
E R L C U R S E D K C D R
N O I T A L U P I N A M I
T I Y T F G J L K F C X F
S E W F U B H T Y K M H I
Y G F B L A C K M A G I C
L K M N Y F L F D X D F E
```

BLACK MAGIC   MALEFICENT

CURSED   MANIPULATION

FORBIDDEN   POISON

DEMONIC   SACRIFICE

RITUAL

Hidden word

Can you find the nine-letter word hidden in the grid?

L	M	Y
B	O	I
S	M	S

Sudoku

Complete the following grid by filling in the empty boxes with the missing numbers. Each number can only appear once in a row, column or box.

4			2		3			
3					6			2
9	2	6	7		5		3	8
	9	7			4	2	6	
			6	7		8	4	
6				8		5		7
			3			7		4
		1	9				8	6
		3						9

Crossword

TAROT

Across

4. This romantic card depicts two amorous people (6)

5. The second trump card was originally called "The Popess" (4, 9)

6. This ominous-sounding card isn't always as negative as it sounds (5)

Down

1. This lucky card is also the name of a television game show (5, 2, 7)

2. The first trump card is named after a performer of illusions (8)

3. This card is named after a person who retreats from society (6)

Maze

Can you help light the candle
with the match?

Word ladder

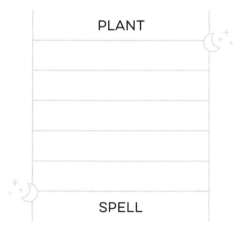

PLANT

SPELL

Change one letter at a
time to turn the word
PLANT into **SPELL**.

Word search

MIND OVER MATTER

```
E  N  L  I  G  H  T  E  N  M  E  N  T  F  T  E
C  P  N  O  I  T  I  N  G  O  C  O  R  T  E  R
N  I  J  L  M  G  Y  E  A  S  W  Q  I  H  V  F
A  T  T  R  A  N  S  C  E  N  D  E  N  T  A  L
Y  D  A  Z  H  Y  F  V  G  H  B  V  Y  H  K  M
O  S  H  A  P  E  S  H  I  F  T  I  N  G  L  F
V  K  J  L  M  B  H  U  Y  D  X  S  E  O  H  B
E  G  U  K  P  L  J  N  B  C  F  T  S  D  X  H
R  F  J  T  E  L  E  K  I  N  E  S  I  S  H  U
I  G  C  D  X  F  H  I  K  L  O  I  H  G  V  Y
A  S  T  R  A  L  P  R  O  J  E  C  T  I  O  N
L  E  V  I  T  A  T  I  O  N  V  J  H  I  K  N
C  H  Y  G  F  G  N  I  D  A  E  R  D  N  I  M
```

ASTRAL PROJECTION   RETROCOGNITION

CLAIRVOYANCE   SHAPESHIFTING

ENLIGHTENMENT   TELEKINESIS

TRANSCENDENTAL   LEVITATION

MIND-READING

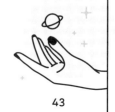

Spot the difference

Can you spot five differences between the two pictures?

(moon) + (moon) + (moon) = 12

((moon) × (moon)) + (ox) = 26

(ox) + ((ox) × (crescent)) = 100

(ox) + (ox) + ((crescent) × (moon)) = _____

Anagrams 46

Rearrange these letters to reveal five phases of the moon.

ACCENTING WRENS   _____

LOOM FLUN   _____

BIGWIG AX BONUS   _____

RAFTER SQUIRT   _____

NO WOMEN   _____

Match up these pairs of seeing eyes. The first one has been done for you.

Word ladder

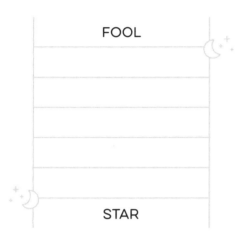

FOOL

STAR

Change one letter at a time to turn the word **FOOL** into **STAR**.

Anagrams

Rearrange these letters to reveal five plants and herbs used for magic.

GUT WORM   _____

AGES   _____

RAVE VIN   _____

EVER LAND   _____

MORE RAYS   _____

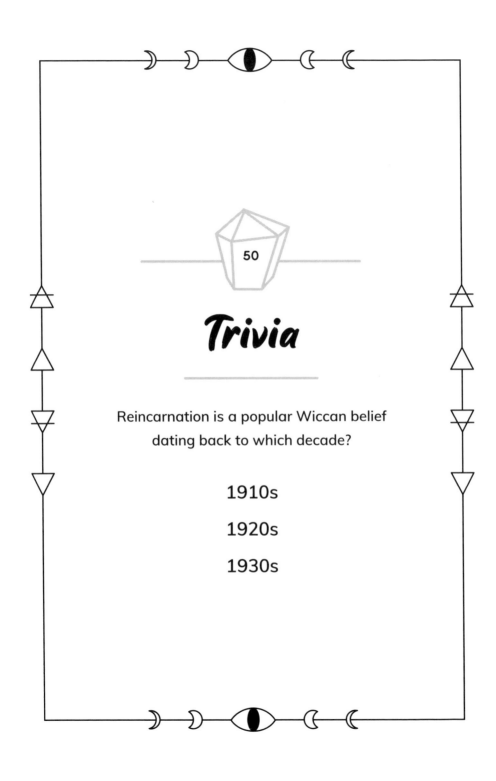

50

Trivia

Reincarnation is a popular Wiccan belief
dating back to which decade?

1910s

1920s

1930s

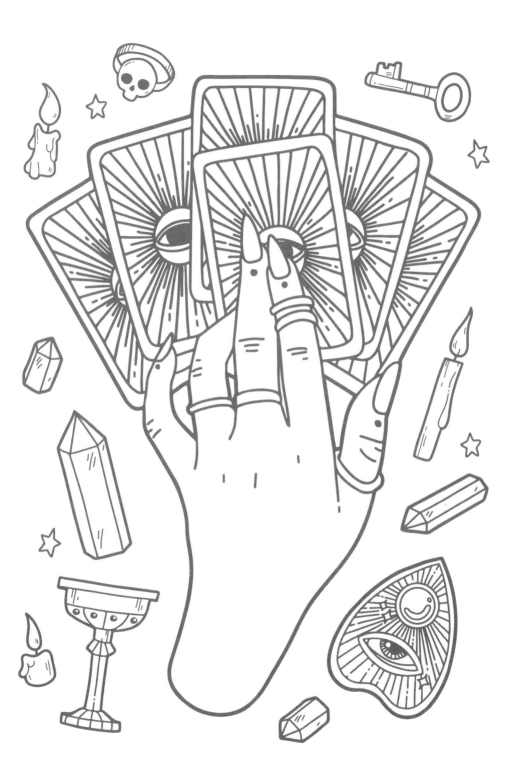

Counting conundrum

▲ + ▲ = 14

● + ■ = 18

● + ▲ = 13

▲ = _____   ● = _____   ■ = _____

Sudoku

Complete the following grid by filling in the empty boxes with the missing numbers. Each number can only appear once in a row, column or box.

9		5			3	2	7	4
	4				7	8		
		7					9	1
	7		2	9	1	4	6	8
	6	4				7	1	9
8	9	1		6	4			2
	5	2					8	6
6	1			5			4	
	3		8	7	6	1		

Acrostics

Solve the clues correctly, and the shaded squares reveal a close-knit group.

1. Leather school bag
2. Metal potion pot
3. Poe's black bird
4. Sight is one of your five…
5. A sign of something to come

Missing link

Fill in the blank spaces to make two compound words or phrases.

WINTER		DROP
FULL		LIGHT
LOOKING		JAR

Spot the difference

Can you spot five differences between the two pictures?

Riddle

All the statements are true – how can that
be if there are only six graves?

Here lie two faithful husbands
with their two loving wives

Here lie two grandmothers with
their two granddaughters

Here lie two dads with
their two daughters

Here lie two mums and their two sons

Here lie two maidens and
their two mothers

Here lie two sisters and two brothers

All were born
legitimately

Word search

ANGELS

```
J  B  V  C  D  S  A  H  R  G  U  J  K
L  M  N  B  H  F  E  D  S  H  J  K  W
U  Q  H  G  D  A  S  W  U  J  G  M  I
C  V  K  I  V  G  L  S  X  P  I  K  N
G  R  V  E  S  E  B  O  F  H  T  R  G
B  G  N  T  I  D  S  Z  P  J  U  E  S
F  L  R  R  C  D  S  A  J  B  G  G  P
Y  K  B  V  G  R  R  C  X  S  H  N  U
J  A  T  C  H  E  R  U  B  I  M  E  R
G  S  A  W  S  L  M  N  V  G  T  S  K
I  D  S  X  T  Y  V  F  D  L  M  S  H
M  I  C  H  A  E  L  W  G  V  C  E  E
W  S  G  U  A  R  D  I  A  N  I  M  N
```

CHERUBIM	MICHAEL
HEAVENLY	MESSENGER
GABRIEL	SERAPHIM
GUARDIAN	WINGS
HALO	

Acrostics

Solve the clues correctly, and the shaded squares will reveal something to move spirits.

1. A clergyman and chess piece
2. Contains all existing matter
3. On a star or with a genie
4. The green-eyed monster
5. Long-eared animal of the Chinese zodiac

Hidden word

Can you find the nine-letter word hidden in the grid?

Y	A	L
P	I	M
S	R	T

Sudoku

Complete the following grid by filling in the empty boxes with the missing numbers. Each number can only appear once in a row, column or box.

		9	6		3		8	
1	3	8	5	7	2	6	9	4
			9					1
				5	9			7
6		3		7	1			5
		5		4	2	3	8	
3				6	5	2		
	9	2		5	1	4	7	
5				9	8	1	3	

Crossword

FULL MOON RITUAL

Across

1. A waxy light that is charged with your intention (6)
4. A type of symbol used in magic and full moon rituals (5)
5. When witches perform rituals naked, they are said to be _____ (7)
6. Asking the universe for what you want and being open to receiving it (13)

Down

2. A positive statement read aloud to support your intention (11)
3. A period of deep thought on your hopes and desires (10)

Maze

Find the right path to locate the crystal ball at the centre of the maze.

Word search

ALIEN ENCOUNTERS

```
O  P  K  M  M  B  V  E  H  M  U  H  T  Q  T  E
F  F  C  V  A  H  F  G  G  U  J  K  U  O  C  L
L  G  F  G  F  R  O  S  W  E  L  L  K  U  V  C
Y  T  K  K  J  N  T  C  G  C  G  U  N  M  J  R
I  G  C  F  H  J  F  I  G  A  C  F  G  U  H  I
N  O  I  T  C  U  D  B  A  F  G  V  H  A  K  C
G  K  J  L  H  B  H  V  Y  N  X  N  E  M  G  P
S  P  A  C  E  C  R  A  F  T  G  J  K  U  U  O
A  L  J  H  Y  H  E  Y  G  H  F  C  V  A  H  R
U  Y  F  D  G  H  J  P  O  J  G  J  C  X  G  C
C  H  G  E  N  O  Y  T  F  I  F  A  E  R  A  D
E  X  T  R  A  T  E  R  R  E  S  T  R  I  A  L
R  K  N  B  G  H  K  I  D  U  Y  G  F  N  Y  M
```

ABDUCTION

AREA FIFTY-ONE

CROP CIRCLE

FLYING SAUCER

EXTRATERRESTRIAL

MARTIAN

OUMUAMUA

ROSWELL

SPACECRAFT

Spot the difference

Can you spot five differences between the two pictures?

Counting conundrum

$$🐍 + 🐍 + 🐍 + 🐍 = 80$$

$$🐍 + 🦎 + 🦎 + 🦎 + 🦎 = 84$$

$$🐌 + 🐌 - 🦎 = 10$$

$$🐍 + (🐌 × 🦎) = \underline{\hphantom{xxxx}}$$

Anagrams

Rearrange these letters to reveal the five things related to Dracula.

PAVE RIM   _____

EMBARK SORT   _____

SALTY NIRVANAI   _____

GLEN VANISH   _____

BY WITH   _____

Pairs

Match up these zodiac symbols. The first pair has been done for you.

♏   ♑

♐   ♓

♌   ♏

♉   ♎

♈   ♉

♋   ♌

♍   ♈

♓   ♋

♎   ♐

♑   ♍

The world could always use a little more magic

Crossword

MYSTICAL CREATURES

Across

2. A tiny, winged creature that lives in the forest (5)

3. A female demon who will try to seduce you in your dreams (8)

6. A serpentine water monster that grows two new heads for each that is cut off (5)

Down

1. A female spirit known for her wailing (7)

4. A figure from Greek mythology – top half human, bottom half horse (7)

5. The serpent king who can kill an enemy with a single glance (8)

Hidden word

Can you find the nine-letter word hidden in the grid?

O	O	Y
T	R	S
A	L	G

Word ladder

HALO

WING

Change one letter at a time to turn the word **HALO** into **WING**.

Counting conundrum

🌙 + 🌙 + 🌙 = 30

🌙 + ☀️ + ☀️ = 18

☀️ − 🌕 = 2

½ 🌕 + (🌙 × ☀️) =

Sudoku

Complete the following grid by filling in the empty boxes with the missing numbers. Each number can only appear once in a row, column or box.

2	1					9	5	
	5			1	7		9	2
	9	7	5	6			4	
5	3				6	2	8	
								3
	2	9		3		4		
				8		3		9
9			6		3			4
	7		2	9	4			5

Anagrams

Rearrange these letters to reveal five creatures from folklore across the world.

RUNE CHAPEL

I RAMMED

HA MERCI

CAT SQUASH

FLOWER WE

Missing link

Fill in the blank spaces to make two compound words or phrases.

CRYSTAL		GOWN
BLACK		WAND
TAROT		GLASSES

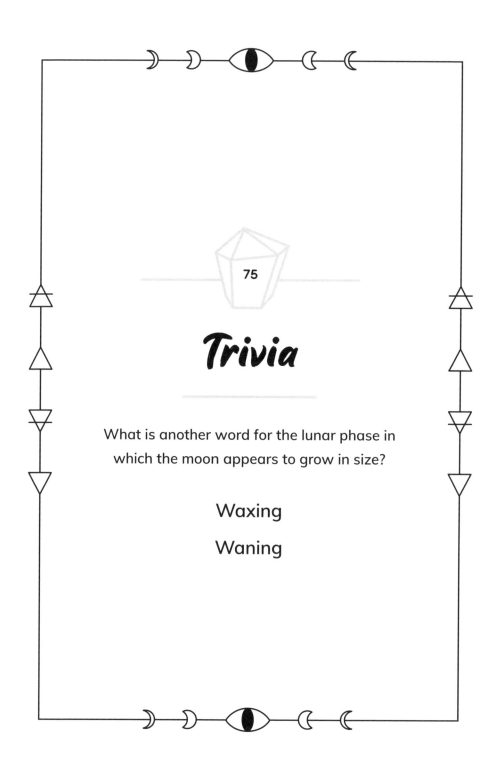

75

Trivia

What is another word for the lunar phase in
which the moon appears to grow in size?

Waxing

Waning

Pairs

Match up these spiritual symbols. The first pair has been done for you.

Maze

Can you help the owl find the tree?

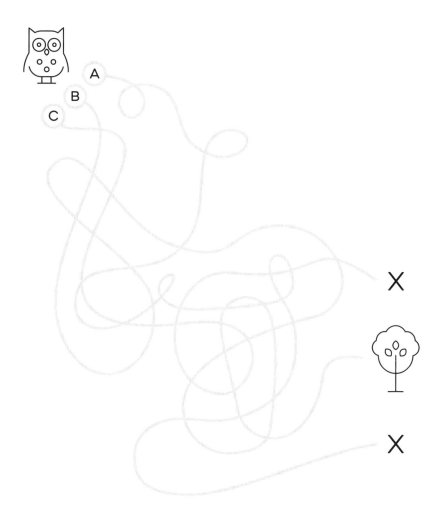

Acrostics

Solve the clues correctly, and the shaded squares will reveal the name of a modern Pagan religion.

1. Cinderella needs to wear one

2. The final season

3. A waxy block with a wick

4. A fine fabric often used in underwear

5. Natural stones with unique properties

Anagrams

Rearrange these letters to reveal five celestial bodies.

NEVUS

RIPE JUT

CURRY ME

NU ARTS

SAU RUN

Spot the difference

Can you spot five differences between the two pictures?

Crossword

BELIEF SYSTEMS

Across

2. A type of doll into which pins are inserted (6)

5. Its followers worship the Devil (8)

6. This South Asian philosophy is often associated with sex and the musician Sting (6)

Down

1. One of the world's largest religions founded around enlightenment more than 2,500 years ago (8)

3. A red string bracelet is the sign of a follower of this mystical interpretation of Judaism (8)

4. A form of modern paganism popular with those who practise witchcraft (5)

Acrostics

Solve the clues correctly, and the shaded squares will reveal the name of a heavenly visitor.

1. Reading the hands to tell the future
2. The cheeky seventh planet
3. Attracts metal
4. The lion sign of the zodiac
5. Magicians and witches cast these

Word search

GODDESSES

```
O  J  N  B  V  C  D  F  F  I  L  O  N
B  P  T  F  X  V  J  R  D  S  J  M  H
R  Y  U  N  B  M  I  N  E  R  V  A  P
G  N  U  T  F  G  S  E  W  Z  B  M  A
Y  E  K  M  G  G  Y  T  B  F  D  I  P
L  M  F  R  E  V  C  I  N  Y  E  W  A
J  E  L  H  R  F  X  A  B  U  H  A  T
E  S  Q  A  L  I  N  M  H  Y  F  T  U
Q  I  J  F  S  Y  P  A  E  C  J  A  A
H  S  C  H  E  C  A  T  E  D  G  A  N
M  B  T  F  W  Y  D  S  G  H  Y  T  U
S  A  D  J  S  E  K  H  M  E  T  B  K
R  T  G  Q  W  I  U  H  C  L  A  D  U
```

FRIGG   NEMESIS

HECATE   PAPATUANUKU

ISHTAR   SEKHMET

MAMI WATA   TIAMAT

MINERVA

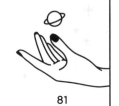

Missing link

Fill in the blank spaces to make two compound words or phrases.

POCKET		FAIR
FIRST		BIRD
MAGIC		BOUND

Spot the difference

84... 85

Can you spot five differences between the two pictures?

Counting conundrum

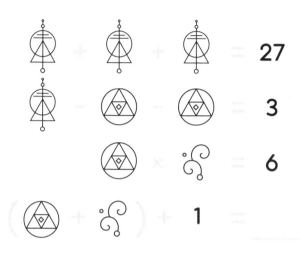

Anagrams

Rearrange these letters to reveal five tarot cards.

PRESS ME

HATPIN HERO

AT CHOIR

MANNED HAG

TEEN CAMPER

Maze

Find the right path to locate the key at the centre of the maze.

Trust your
intuition

Crossword

TELLING THE FUTURE

Across

2. A tasty treat at the end of a Chinese meal that could spell good luck or bad (7, 6)

4. The study of reading the inside of the hand for life indicators (9)

5. The name for someone gifted with the ability to see into the future (11)

Down

1. The act of looking into a reflective object or surface to detect visions or messages (7)

3. A glass orb traditionally used by clairvoyants (7, 4)

6. Using a deck of 78 cards, including 22 Major Arcana, to see what is yet to come (5)

Word wheel

See how many words of four or more letters you can make, using each letter only once. Each word must use the central letter. Can you find a word that uses all of the letters?

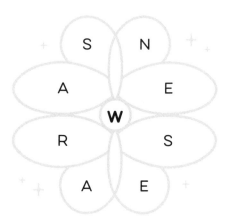

Word ladder

BEAM

Change one letter at a time to turn the word **BEAM** into **GLOW**.

GLOW

Pairs

Match up these feathers. The first pair has been done for you.

Acrostics

Solve the clues correctly, and the shaded squares will reveal the name of a rather special deck of cards.

1. Map out your life with a birth ___
2. The ram sign of the zodiac
3. Blood-sucking creature
4. Soothing herb and calming tea
5. The art of moving objects with your mind

Spot the difference

Can you spot five differences between the two pictures?

Missing link

Fill in the blank spaces to make two compound words or phrases.

RISING		SALUTATION
MORNING		BEADS
BEAUTY		WALKING

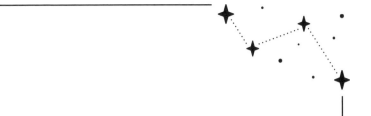

Riddle

Can you solve this riddle?

I can't be seen, touched,
heard or smelled.

I live behind stars and
fill empty holes.

What am I?

Word search

SUPERNATURAL BEINGS

```
K B C F S W R H B X Z A G
P U I K L M G N O G A R D
W A P H O E N I X F J I T
E Q A Z C D G B Y J N K I
T S I E G R E T L O P X H
Y G U J B K Y F R D S Z X
M R H C K A H Y R D S O E
E I S C C Y N A K B C G R
R F N U Y U D S Y P K H I
M F C G T Y B S H G Y H P
A I H V Y T H U L E U G M
I N W F H N J I S V E G A
D J F I R E B I R D R W V
```

BANSHEE	PHOENIX
DRAGON	POLTERGEIST
FIREBIRD	SUCCUBUS
GRIFFIN	VAMPIRE
MERMAID	

Missing link

Fill in the blank spaces to make two compound words or phrases.

LUCKY		BRACELET
WHITE		DOCTOR
FALLING		SIGN

Anagrams

Rearrange these letters to reveal five famous witches from history.

MORPHINE SHOTT

GARGLED ERRAND

NEVER TOENAILEDI

SAND RELAXES

AERIAL MAUVE

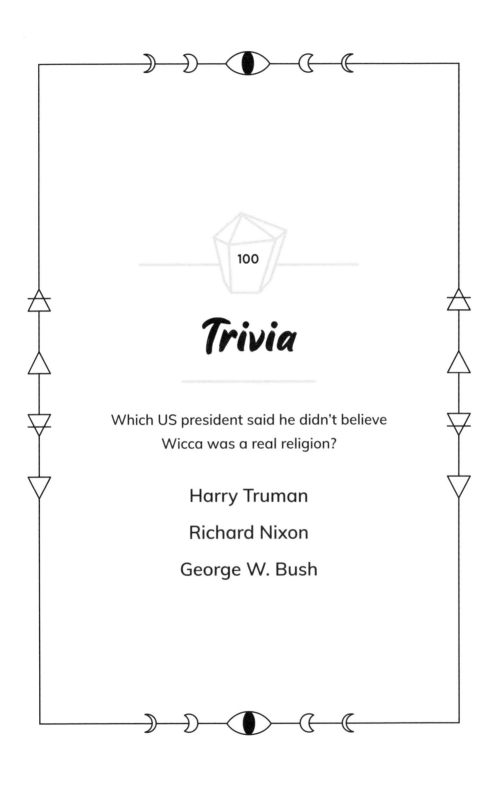

100

Trivia

Which US president said he didn't believe
Wicca was a real religion?

Harry Truman

Richard Nixon

George W. Bush

Hidden word

Can you find the nine-letter word hidden in the grid?

B	E	I
N	I	V
I	S	L

Word ladder

Change one letter at a time to turn the word **WISE** into **YOGI**.

WISE

YOGI

Acrostics

Solve the clues correctly, and the shaded squares will reveal the Wiccan name for the summer solstice.

1. Find a penny for good...
2. Believers and George Michael have it
3. A dwarf planet and Mickey's dog
4. A medium or seer
5. The bull sign of the zodiac

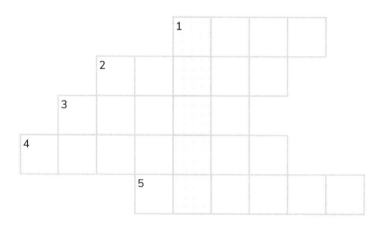

Crossword

SPIRITS

Across

1. This archdemon tempts humans to commit the sin of pride (7)
5. A spooky presence that can move objects (11)
6. This shapeshifting being is famous in stories for granting wishes (5)

Down

2. The removal of demonic possession in the Catholic Church, made famous by a 1970s horror film (8)
3. A supernatural spirit often believed to be sent by a deity to look over us (5)
4. A flying demon who features in the lyrics of Queen's "Bohemian Rhapsody" (9)

Sudoku

Complete the following grid by filling in the empty boxes with the missing numbers. Each number can only appear once in a row, column or box.

7					8			1
	3	1	4	7	2		5	8
			3			2	4	7
	5					4	8	
		2	8				3	
8				5		1		9
2								4
			2		4	6		
	9				8	5		

Maze

Can you help get the herbs into the cauldron?

A

B

C

Counting conundrum

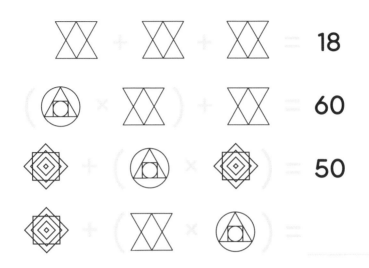

$$\boxtimes + \boxtimes + \boxtimes = 18$$

$$(\circledtriangle \times \boxtimes) + \boxtimes = 60$$

$$\diamondsuit + (\circledtriangle \times \diamondsuit) = 50$$

$$\diamondsuit + (\boxtimes \times \circledtriangle) =$$

Anagrams

Rearrange these letters to reveal five fortune-telling methods.

AMPLY STIR

ART TO

STORY GOAL

AGHAST OSPREY

Word ladder

WILD

PATH

Change one letter at a time to turn the word **WILD** into **PATH**.

Anagrams

Rearrange these letters to reveal five things you might find at a séance.

A BIJOU ROAD

NINE SEC

DUNE LUMP

TIP SIR

EMU MID

Word search

OUTER SPACE

```
N  G  C  X  A  W  S  R  G  Y  H  U  C
D  K  J  U  B  G  V  F  P  L  R  H  O
E  D  C  E  L  E  S  T  I  A  L  Q  A
E  U  H  G  A  D  X  L  N  M  H  U  J
T  B  V  F  C  Y  P  U  K  I  U  H  U
I  W  A  G  K  C  S  T  Y  W  S  Z  P
L  B  V  Y  H  H  I  P  P  L  K  M  I
L  G  D  F  O  Y  G  A  L  A  X  Y  T
E  C  H  G  L  Y  U  J  A  B  P  L  E
T  D  I  H  E  A  W  G  N  H  B  J  R
A  M  N  H  G  C  F  R  E  K  U  H  C
S  O  L  A  R  S  Y  S  T  E  M  P  K
J  F  G  V  Y  M  E  R  C  U  R  Y  P
```

BLACK HOLE	PLANET
CELESTIAL	SATELLITE
GALAXY	SOLAR SYSTEM
JUPITER	URANUS
MERCURY	

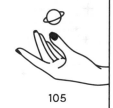

Crossword

WITCHCRAFT

Across

2. A large metal pot used to hold the ingredients for an elixir or potion (8)

3. An object, often sacred, that has been charged with a specific purpose (8)

4. This trusted companion is actually a lower demon in the guise of an animal (8)

5. A witch's bible, filled with rituals, recipes and spells (4, 2, 7)

Down

1. This is the spell you read aloud; the series of words to make it happen (11)

6. Like spices, these aromatic plants are also used in spells and potions (5)

Word wheel

See how many words of four or more letters you can make, using each letter only once. Each word must use the central letter. Can you find a word that uses all of the letters?

Word ladder

FIRE

RAIN

Change one letter at a time to turn the word **FIRE** into **RAIN**.

Maze

Find the right path to locate the mirror at the centre of the maze.

Crossword

PALM READING

Across

3. Different hand shapes are named after the four elements: earth, fire, air and _____ (5)

5. This fleshy area located at the base of the thumb is linked to love and sensuality (5, 2, 5)

6. There are two lines on the hand that represent parts of the body. One is the head, the other is the _____ (5)

Down

1. This major line reveals your experiences, vitality and zest (4, 4)

2. Which word of Greek origin is another word for palmistry? (10)

4. This line is named for the star in our solar system (3, 4)

117

Riddle

Can you solve this riddle?

What building has the most stories?

Word search

CRYSTALS

```
G  B  I  J  M  O  O  N  S  T  O  N  E
A  E  S  K  I  H  V  G  Y  D  X  S  W
M  J  Q  F  Y  B  M  J  N  K  E  L  T
E  X  S  U  Q  J  A  S  P  E  R  T  I
T  C  X  O  A  H  U  Y  N  C  I  R  G
H  K  N  G  U  R  G  O  Y  H  H  L  E
Y  D  X  T  Y  V  T  A  Q  Z  P  U  R
S  B  K  I  J  S  F  Z  Y  B  P  C  S
T  O  M  B  D  D  S  B  C  T  A  G  E
U  I  P  O  J  F  S  Q  A  X  S  G  Y
I  G  O  B  S  I  D  I  A  N  J  L  E
H  L  V  Y  R  S  F  X  F  V  H  U  J
B  L  Q  T  U  R  Q  U  O  I  S  E  U
```

AMETHYST	SAPPHIRE
BLOODSTONE	TIGER'S EYE
JASPER	TURQUOISE
MOONSTONE	QUARTZ
OBSIDIAN	

Spot the difference

Can you spot five differences between the two pictures?

Acrostics

Solve the clues correctly, and the shaded squares will reveal something we could all use a little more of.

1. The periodic table is made up of...
2. The red planet
3. Burn this herb for purification
4. From the sun, the moon, or a bulb
5. Throw them for a number from one to six

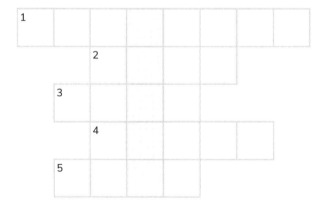

Word ladder

HERB

SAGE

Change one letter at a time to turn the word **HERB** into **SAGE**.

Anagrams

Rearrange these letters to reveal five signs of the zodiac.

RAISE

SPICES

COIR OPS

AGA STIR SUIT

BRAIL

Pairs

Match up the crystals. The first pair has been done for you.

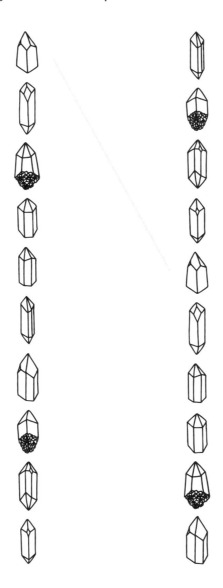

Counting conundrum

$$\text{✦} + \text{☀} = 13$$

$$\text{✦} \times \text{☀} = 42$$

$$\text{✦} - \text{☀} = 1$$

$$\text{✦} = \quad\quad \text{☀} =$$

Sudoku

Complete the following grid by filling in the empty boxes with the missing numbers. Each number can only appear once in a row, column or box.

		7	4		9		8	1
8			3		1		4	
		1						2
7		3		4	6	9		5
	5		2		7			6
			1	3	5			8
9		4	7				6	3
3					4	1		
		6		1				

Missing link

Fill in the blank spaces to make two compound words or phrases.

SATANIC		DANCE
FAIRY		BACK
FALLEN		WINGS

Hidden word

Can you find the nine-letter word hidden in the grid?

J	G	I
N	R	O
U	N	C

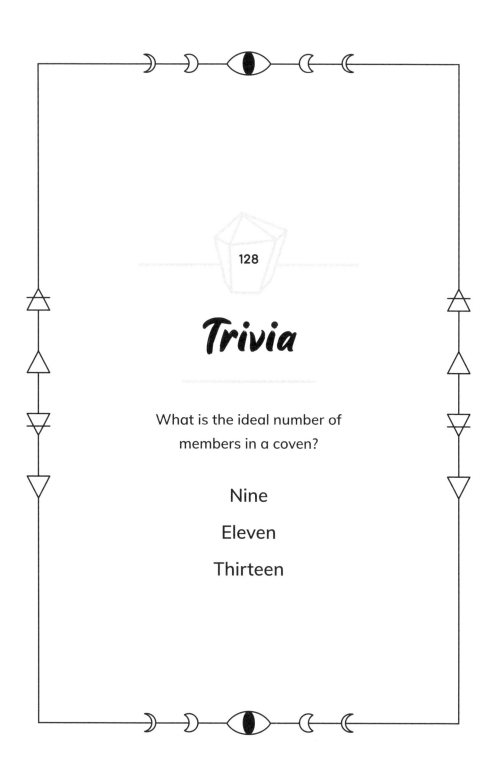

128

Trivia

What is the ideal number of
members in a coven?

Nine

Eleven

Thirteen

Cosmic shifts
are coming
your way

Word wheel

See how many words of four
or more letters you can make,
using each letter only once.
Each word must use the central
letter. Can you find a word
that uses all of the letters?

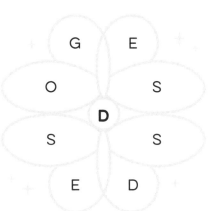

G E
O S
D
S S
E D

Word ladder

MOON

RUNE

Change one letter at a
time to turn the word
MOON into **RUNE**.

Word search

SIGNS OF THE ZODIAC

```
J  C  O  P  H  D  E  Q  Y  A  F  C  C
K  S  A  K  O  I  U  F  B  P  K  H  A
S  A  G  I  T  T  A  R  I  U  S  H  P
O  G  Q  L  J  F  C  R  R  E  T  U  R
A  M  N  U  L  L  H  G  I  Y  F  X  I
S  P  U  H  A  G  T  K  I  E  C  D  C
Y  I  L  J  V  R  E  V  A  T  S  O  O
G  S  B  V  T  U  I  G  A  D  E  K  R
E  C  Y  F  C  R  E  U  H  Y  F  V  N
M  E  M  N  G  H  R  C  S  E  S  D  Y
I  S  F  O  J  U  G  Y  J  K  L  L  M
N  I  G  V  S  D  S  C  O  R  P  I  O
I  V  C  Z  X  D  R  E  S  F  H  Q  A
```

ARIES	SAGITTARIUS
AQUARIUS	SCORPIO
CAPRICORN	TAURUS
GEMINI	VIRGO
PISCES	

Acrostics

Solve the clues correctly, and the shaded squares will reveal one of the four elements.

1. Using a rod to find water

2. The crab sign of the zodiac

3. The study of star signs

4. A star with five points

5. A reflective glass surface

Rearrange these letters to reveal five tarot cards.

AGAIN MIC

OW EFFLUENT HERO

SOLVER

THE RIM

POEM ERR

Sudoku

Complete the following grid by filling in the empty boxes with the missing numbers. Each number can only appear once in a row, column or box.

5	3		7	1	9	6		
4		9				5	1	7
	7	1		6			3	2
			2	4	6			
3	9	6				4	2	8
	4	7						6
			9	2		6		
9			6	7		4		
6	2		4					

Crossword

HERBS AND REMEDIES

Across

2. A fragrant wood that, when burned, is known to get rid of negative energy (5)

3. A type of stick that is burned during meditation and spellcasting (7)

5. This soothing herb, popular in tea, is used for healing, happiness and relieving stress (9)

6. This herb is often burned for smudging, cleansing and purification (4)

Down

1. A potent herb from Malaysia that is often used in spellcasting (9)

4. Often paired with thyme, this herb is hung in bundles on the door to protect the inhabitants from harm (8)

Maze

Can you help the witch find the
Book of Shadows?

A

B

C

Word ladder

CARD

Change one letter at a
time to turn the word
CARD into **LUCK**.

LUCK

Hidden word

Can you find the nine-letter word hidden in the grid?

P	G	A
N	A	M
T	E	R

Spot the difference

Can you spot five differences between the two pictures?

Counting conundrum

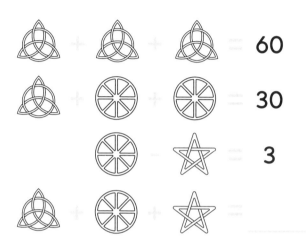

Anagrams

Rearrange these letters to reveal five crystals.

I GREET YES

ADIOS BIN

SUE OR QUIT

ME ONTO SON

AIM TEETH

Maze

Find the right path to locate the *Book of Shadows* at the centre of the maze.

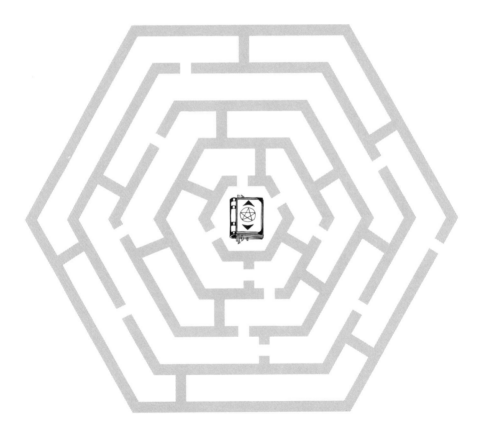

Pairs

Match up the rune symbols. The first pair has been done for you.

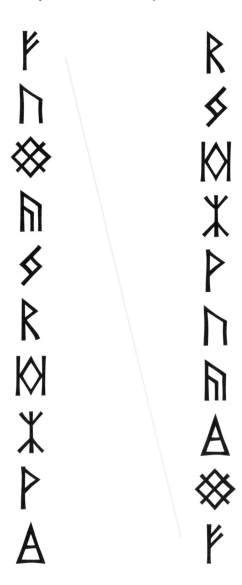

Word ladder

LUNAR

RIVER

Change one letter at a
time to turn the word
LUNAR into **RIVER**.

Anagrams

Rearrange these letters to reveal five types of meditation.

CANDLE RAN TENTS

DIMS FUNNELS

INCH GNAT

VENOM MET

RACK AH

Meditate on your dreams – then make your move

Word wheel

See how many words of four or more letters you can make, using each letter only once. Each word must use the central letter. Can you find a word that uses all of the letters?

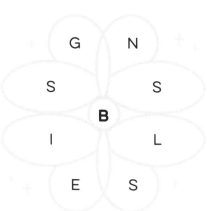

Word ladder

SAGE

Change one letter at a time to turn the word **SAGE** into **HEAL**.

HEAL

Counting conundrum

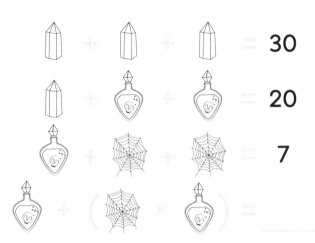

= 30

= 20

= 7

Sudoku

Complete the following grid by filling in the empty boxes with the missing numbers. Each number can only appear once in a row, column or box.

	6	2					3	7
	8			4	6			1
	1	5	3		2	9		6
8		1	7	3				
3								
5			4	2	8		1	3
	5	8	6		7		9	
				5				
		7	8			5		2

Crossword

MYSTICAL PLACES

Across

2. This mythical lost world is a paradise hidden in the ocean (8)

5. This Polish woodland has oddly shaped pine trees that cannot be explained (7, 6)

6. This prehistoric monument on Salisbury Plain is particularly popular during summer solstice or 'Litha' (10)

Down

1. This spiritual pilgrimage site is better known to the wide world for its festival (11)

3. This large block of limestone in Ireland is said to be lucky if you kiss it (7, 5)

4. The ancient stony faces are the most famous inhabitants of this spot in the Pacific Ocean (6, 6)

Can you spot five differences between the two pictures?

Word search

SPELLCASTING

```
J  C  O  P  H  D  E  Q  Y  A  F  C  C
L  A  U  T  I  R  U  F  B  P  K  H  A
C  E  R  E  M  O  N  Y  C  I  S  H  U
O  G  Q  L  J  F  C  R  R  N  T  U  L
A  M  N  U  L  L  H  G  Y  C  F  X  D
S  P  U  H  A  G  T  K  S  A  C  D  R
Y  I  L  J  H  R  E  V  T  N  S  O  O
M  A  N  I  F  E  S  T  A  T  I  O  N
E  C  Y  F  C  R  R  U  L  A  F  V  N
M  E  M  N  G  H  R  B  S  T  S  D  Y
I  S  F  O  J  U  G  Y  S  I  L  L  M
N  I  G  V  S  N  O  I  T  O  P  I  O
C  A  N  D  L  E  S  E  S  N  H  Q  A
```

CANDLES	INCANTATION
CAULDRON	MANIFESTATION
CEREMONY	POTION
CRYSTALS	RITUAL
HERBS	

Answers

01: Sagittarius, Cancer, Gemini, Leo, Pisces, Taurus

02: a pair of dice

03:

04:

05: haiku, meditate, fortune, amethyst, Libra = karma

06: star – stat – stet – suet – duet – dust

07: amethyst, garnet, selenite, citrine, tourmaline

08:

09:

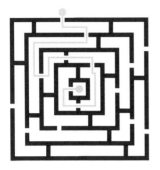

10:

⊛ = 15, 木 = 10, ૐ = 5;

15 − 5 + 10 = 20

11:

4	6	1	3	7	2	5	8	9
9	2	5	1	4	8	6	7	3
3	8	7	6	9	5	2	1	4
8	9	4	5	1	7	3	6	2
1	3	6	8	2	4	9	5	7
5	7	2	9	3	6	1	4	8
6	5	3	4	8	9	7	2	1
2	1	8	7	6	3	4	9	5
7	4	9	2	5	1	8	3	6

12: wish, dream, planet

13: horoscope

14: nine-letter word = vibration; other words = anti, bait, boat, bort, bota, brat, brit, inti, into, iota, nota, rant, riot, rota, roti, tarn, taro, tori, torn, trio, vita, abort, baton, biota, brant, intro, nitro, orbit, ratio, riant, tabor, tibia, torii, train, trona, biotin, obtain, ration, trivia, vibrant, vibrato

15: full – fill – mill – mild – mold – mood - moon

16:

17: cast, spider, electric, umbrella, laugh = spell

18: herbalist

19:

6	1	7	4	2	8	5	9	3
3	9	5	7	1	6	8	2	4
4	2	8	3	5	9	1	7	6
2	5	6	1	8	4	9	3	7
9	7	4	6	3	5	2	1	8
8	3	1	9	7	2	4	6	5
5	8	3	2	9	7	6	4	1
1	6	2	5	4	3	7	8	9
7	4	9	8	6	1	3	5	2

20: amethyst, rose quartz, black tourmaline, selenite, citrine, jade

21: A

22: wild – wind – bind – band – hand – hard – card

23: three

24:

25:

 = 8, = 9, =4

26: cauldron, herbs, altar, pentagram, potion

27:

28: tarot – taros – tarts – carts – cards

29: air, spirit, water, earth, fire

30: nine-letter word = spiritual; other words = alps, laps, lipa, lips, lisp, pail, pair, pals, pars, part, past, pats, pial. pits, plat, plus, prat, prau, ptui, pula, puri, purl, puts, raps, rapt, rasp, rips, slap, slip, spar, spat, spit, spur, taps, tarp, tips, trap, trip, tups, upas, lapis, pails, pairs, parts, pilar, pilau, pilus, plait, plats, prats, praus, puris, purls, sirup, slurp, spilt, spirt, splat, split, sprat, sprit, spurt, sputa, strap, strip, stupa, supra, tapir, tapis, tarps, traps, trips, tulip, turps, uplit, pistil, plaits, pulsar, purist, rapist, spiral, spirit, spruit, tapirs, tulips, stipular

31: sleep – bleep – bleed – breed – bread – bream – dream

32:

= 10, = 5, = 4;

10 + (5 x 4) = 30

33:

2	7	3	5	9	4	6	8	1
1	8	6	2	3	7	5	4	9
9	5	4	6	8	1	7	2	3
8	2	9	4	1	5	3	6	7
3	6	1	8	7	9	4	5	2
7	4	5	3	2	6	1	9	8
4	1	7	9	5	8	2	3	6
6	3	8	7	4	2	9	1	5
5	9	2	1	6	3	8	7	4

34: zodiac, Venus, houses, moon, Mars, astrology

35:

36:

37:

M	H	B	F	O	R	B	I	D	D	E	N	M
A	Y	L	J	D	V	C	F	R	E	O	D	J
L	Z	Y	H	G	E	F	R	D	S	A	Z	C
E	H	Y	J	A	K	M	L	I	J	N	B	V
F	Y	G	V	C	C	K	O	H	B	V	C	S
I	X	S	G	H	Y	P	D	N	J	A	X	A
C	Z	M	N	B	H	Y	G	D	I	G	Y	C
E	R	L	C	U	R	S	E	D	K	C	D	R
N	O	I	T	A	L	U	P	I	N	A	M	I
T	I	Y	T	F	G	J	L	K	F	C	X	F
S	E	W	F	U	B	H	T	Y	K	M	H	I
Y	G	F	B	L	A	C	K	M	A	G	I	C
L	K	M	N	Y	F	L	F	D	X	D	F	E

38: symbolism

39:

4	7	8	2	9	3	6	1	5
3	1	5	8	4	6	9	7	2
9	2	6	7	1	5	4	3	8
8	9	7	5	3	4	2	6	1
1	5	2	6	7	9	8	4	3
6	3	4	1	8	2	5	9	7
2	8	9	3	6	1	7	5	4
5	4	1	9	2	7	3	8	6
7	6	3	4	5	8	1	2	9

40: Hermit, High Priestess, Lovers, Wheel of Fortune, Death, Magician

41: B

42: plant – slant – scant – scent – spent – spelt – spell

43:

44:

45:

$\left(\ast\right)$ = 4, $\bigcirc$ = 10, $\bigcirc$ =9; 20 + (9 x 4) = 56

46: waning crescent, full moon, waxing gibbous, first quarter, new moon

47:

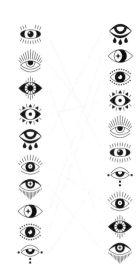

48: fool – foul – soul – soup – soap – soar– star

49: mugwort, sage, vervain, lavender, rosemary

50: 1930s

51:

 = 7, ⬤ = 6, ◼ =12

52:

9	8	5	6	1	3	2	7	4
1	4	6	9	2	7	8	5	3
3	2	7	4	8	5	6	9	1
5	7	3	2	9	1	4	6	8
2	6	4	5	3	8	7	1	9
8	9	1	7	6	4	5	3	2
7	5	2	1	4	9	3	8	6
6	1	8	3	5	2	9	4	7
4	3	9	8	7	6	1	2	5

53: satchel, cauldron, raven, senses, omen = coven

54: snow, moon, glass

55:

56: If two widows, each having married the son of the other widow, each had a daughter, all the statements will be true.

57:

58: bishop, universe, wish, jealousy, rabbit = Oujia

59: palmistry

60:

4	5	9	6	1	3	7	8	2
1	3	8	5	7	2	6	9	4
7	2	6	9	4	8	3	5	1
2	4	1	8	3	5	9	6	7
6	8	3	2	9	7	1	4	5
9	7	5	1	6	4	2	3	8
3	1	4	7	8	6	5	2	9
8	9	2	3	5	1	4	7	6
5	6	7	4	2	9	8	1	3

61: sigil, manifestation, candle, meditation, skyclad, affirmation

62:

63:

64:

65:

🐍 = 20, 🦎 = 16, 🐌 = 13;

20 + (13 x 16) = 228

66: Vampire, Bram Stoker, Transylvania, Van Helsing, Whitby

67:

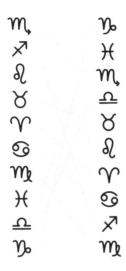

68: succubus, banshee, basilisk, centaur, fairy, Hydra

69: astrology

70: halo – hall – hill – will – wild – wind – wing

71:

= 10, = 4, = 2;
1 + (10 x 4) = 41

72:

2	1	6	8	4	9	5	3	7
4	5	8	3	1	7	6	9	2
3	9	7	5	6	2	1	4	8
5	3	4	9	7	6	2	8	1
8	6	1	4	2	5	9	7	3
7	2	9	1	3	8	4	5	6
6	4	5	7	8	1	3	2	9
9	8	2	6	5	3	7	1	4
1	7	3	2	9	4	8	6	5

73: leprechaun, mermaid, chimera, sasquatch, werewolf

74: ball, magic, reading

75: waxing

76:

77: B

78: ballgown, winter, candle, lace, crystals = Wicca

79: Venus, Jupiter, Mercury, Saturn, Uranus

80:

81: Satanism, Kabbalah, Buddhism, Voodoo, Tantra, Wicca

82: palmistry, Uranus, magnet, Leo, spells = angel

83:

O	J	N	B	V	C	D	F	F	I	L	O	N
B	P	T	F	X	V	J	R	D	S	J	M	H
R	Y	U	N	B	M	I	N	E	R	V	A	P
G	N	U	T	F	G	S	E	W	Z	B	M	A
Y	E	K	M	G	G	Y	T	B	F	D	I	P
L	M	F	R	E	V	C	I	N	Y	E	W	A
J	E	L	H	R	F	X	A	B	U	H	A	T
E	S	Q	A	L	I	N	M	H	Y	F	T	U
Q	I	J	F	S	Y	P	A	E	C	J	A	A
H	S	C	H	E	C	A	T	E	D	G	A	N
M	B	T	F	W	Y	D	S	G	H	Y	T	U
S	A	D	J	S	E	K	H	M	E	T	B	K
R	T	G	Q	W	I	U	H	C	L	A	D	U

84: book, lady, spell

85:

86:

⊕ = 9, △ = 3, ♕ =2;

9 − (3 + 2) + 1 = 5

87: Empress, Hierophant, Chariot, Hanged Man, Temperance

88:

89: fortune cookie, tarot, palmistry, scrying, crystal ball, clairvoyant

90: nine-letter word = awareness; other words = anew, awes, awns, ewer, ewes, news, sawn, saws, sewn, sews, swan, wane, ware, warn, wars, wean, wear, ween, wees, wens, were, wren, aware, ewers, newer, renew, resaw, resew, sewer, swans, swear, wanes, wares, warns, weans, wears, weens, wrens, answer, renews, resaws, resewn, resews, seesaw, sewers, swears, weaner, wrasse, answers, rawness, seaware, weaners, seawares

91: beam – beat – feat – flat – flaw – flow – glow

92:

93: chart, Aries, vampire, chamomile, telekinesis = tarot

94:

95: sun, prayer, sleep

96: darkness

97:

K	B	C	F	S	W	R	H	B	X	Z	A	G
P	U	I	K	L	M	G	N	O	G	A	R	D
W	A	P	H	O	E	N	I	X	F	J	I	T
E	Q	A	Z	C	D	G	B	Y	J	N	K	I
T	S	I	E	G	R	E	T	L	O	P	X	H
Y	G	U	J	B	K	Y	F	R	D	S	Z	X
M	R	H	C	K	A	H	Y	R	D	S	O	E
E	I	S	C	C	Y	N	A	K	B	C	G	R
R	F	N	U	Y	U	D	S	Y	P	K	H	I
M	F	C	G	T	Y	B	S	H	G	Y	H	P
A	I	H	V	Y	T	H	U	L	E	U	G	M
I	N	W	F	H	N	J	I	S	V	E	G	A
D	J	F	I	R	E	B	I	R	D	R	W	V

105:

7	2	4	9	8	5	3	6	1
6	3	1	4	7	2	9	5	8
9	8	5	3	1	6	2	4	7
3	5	9	7	2	1	4	8	6
1	6	2	8	4	9	7	3	5
8	4	7	6	5	3	1	2	9
2	1	3	5	6	7	8	9	4
5	7	8	2	9	4	6	1	3
4	9	6	1	3	8	5	7	2

106: C

98: charm, witch, star

99: Mother Shipton, Gerald Gardner, Doreen Valiente, Alex Sanders, Marie Laveau

100: George W. Bush

101: invisible

102: wise – wire – tire – tore – tora – toga – yoga

103: luck, faith, Pluto, psychic, Taurus = Litha

104: exorcism, angel, poltergeist, Lucifer, genie, Beelzebub

107:

$\bowtie$ = 6, $\oslash$ = 9, $\diamondsuit$ = 5;
5 + (6 x 9) = 59

108: palmistry, tarot, astrology, runes, tasseography

109: wild – wile – pile – pale – pate – path

110: Ouija board, incense, pendulum, spirit, medium

111:

```
N G C X A W S R G Y H U C
D K J U B G V F P L R H O
E D C E L E S T I A L Q A
E U H G A D X L N M H U J
T B V F C Y P U K I U H U
I W A G K C S T Y W S Z P
L B V Y H H I P P L K M I
L G D F O Y G A L A X Y T
E C H G L Y U J A B P L E
T D I H E A W G N H B J R
A M N H G C F R E K U H C
S O L A R S Y S T E M P K
J F G V Y M E R C U R Y P
```

112: Book of Shadows, cauldron, familiar, talisman, herbs, incantation

113: nine-letter word = intuition; other words = inti, into, tint, titi, unio, unit, inion, union, intuit, tuition

114: fire – file – fill – fall – fail – rail – rain

115:

116: heart, Mount of Venus, life line, sun line, water, chiromancy

117: a library

118:

```
G B I J M O O N S T O N E
A E S K I H V G Y D X S W
M J Q F Y B M J N K E L T
E X S U Q J A S P E R T I
T C X O A H U Y N C I R G
H K N G U R G O Y H H L E
Y D X T Y V T A Q Z P U R
S B K I J S F Z Y B P C S
T O M B D D S B C T A G E
U I P O J F S Q A X S G Y
I G O B S I D I A N J L E
H L V Y R S F X F V H U J
B L Q T U R Q U O I S E U
```

119:

120: elements, Mars, sage, light, dice = magic

121: herb – here – hare – ware – wage – sage

122: Aries, Pisces, Scorpio, Sagittarius, Libra

123:

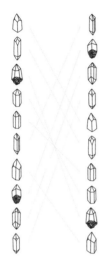

124:

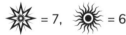 = 7, = 6

125:

2	3	7	4	6	9	5	8	1
8	9	5	3	2	1	6	4	7
4	6	1	5	7	8	3	9	2
7	2	3	8	4	6	9	1	5
1	5	8	2	9	7	4	3	6
6	4	9	1	3	5	2	7	8
9	1	4	7	5	2	8	6	3
3	7	2	6	8	4	1	5	9
5	8	6	9	1	3	7	2	4

126: ritual, circle, angel

127: conjuring

128: 13

129: nine-letter word = Goddesses; other words = deed, does, doge, dogs, dose, doss, eddo, edge, geed, gods, odds, odes, seed, sods, deeds, dodge, doges, dosed, doses, edged, edges, geode, sedge, seeds, dodges, dossed, dosses, eddoes, geodes, sedges, goddess

130: moon – mood – mold – mole – mule – rule – rune

131:

132: dowsing, Cancer, astrology, pentacle, mirror = water

133: Magician, Wheel of Fortune, Lovers, Hermit, Emperor

134:

5	3	2	7	1	9	6	8	4
4	6	9	8	3	2	5	1	7
8	7	1	5	6	4	9	3	2
1	5	8	2	4	6	3	7	9
3	9	6	1	5	7	4	2	8
2	4	7	3	9	8	1	5	6
7	1	4	9	2	3	8	6	5
9	8	3	6	7	5	2	4	1
6	2	5	4	8	1	7	9	3

135: sage, cedar, patchouli, incense, chamomile, rosemary

136: A

137: card – cars – bars – bark – back – buck – luck

138: pentagram

139:

140:

 = 20, = 5, = 2

20 + 5 + 2 = 27

141: tiger's eye, obsidian, turquoise, moonstone, hematite

142:

143:

144: lunar – lunas – lunes – lines – liner – liver – river

145: transcendental, mindfulness, chanting, movement, chakra

146: nine-letter word = blessings; other words = begs, bels, bile, bine, bins, blin, gibe, gibs, glib, libs, nebs, nibs, sibs, snib, begin, being, bilge, bines, binge, bless, bling, bliss, gibes, snibs, begins, beings, bilges, binges, bigness, blisses, blessing, glibness

147: sage – sale – tale – tall – tell – teal – heal

148:

⬙ = 10, 🧪 = 5, 🕸 = 1;
5 + (1 x 5) = 10

149:

9	6	2	5	8	1	4	3	7
7	8	3	9	4	6	2	5	1
4	1	5	3	7	2	9	8	6
8	2	1	7	3	9	6	4	5
3	7	4	1	6	5	8	2	9
5	9	6	4	2	8	7	1	3
2	5	8	6	1	7	3	9	4
6	4	9	2	5	3	1	7	8
1	3	7	8	9	4	5	6	2

150: Glastonbury, Stonehenge, Easter Island, Atlantis, Crooked Forest, Blarney Stone

151:

152:

J	C	O	P	H	D	E	Q	Y	A	F	C	C
L	A	U	T	I	R	U	F	B	P	K	H	A
C	E	R	E	M	O	N	Y	C	I	S	H	U
O	G	Q	L	J	F	C	R	R	N	T	U	L
A	M	N	U	L	L	H	G	Y	C	F	X	D
S	P	U	H	A	G	T	K	S	A	C	D	R
Y	I	L	J	H	R	E	V	T	N	S	O	O
M	A	N	I	F	E	S	T	A	T	I	O	N
E	C	Y	F	C	R	R	U	L	A	F	V	N
M	E	M	N	G	H	R	B	S	T	S	D	Y
I	S	F	O	J	U	G	Y	S	I	L	L	M
N	I	G	V	S	N	O	I	T	O	P	I	O
C	A	N	D	L	E	S	E	S	N	H	Q	A

Image credits

Have you enjoyed this book?
If so, find us on Facebook at
Summersdale Publishers, on Twitter
at **@Summersdale** and on Instagram
at **@summersdalebooks** and get in
touch. We'd love to hear from you!

www.summersdale.com